AN HISTORICAL GUIDE TO
THE SCULPTURES OF THE PARTHENON

The Temporary Elgin Room in 1819 (from an oil-painting by A. Archer, in the British Museum)

The seated figures in the left foreground are Sir Benjamin West (left) and Sir Joseph Planta (Principal Librarian, 1799–1827). On the extreme left, behind the Ilissus, appears Benjamin Robert Haydon; in the right foreground, A. Archer, the artist.

An Historical Guide to
THE SCULPTURES OF
THE PARTHENON

Published by the Trustees of the British Museum
1969

Printed in England by Balding+Mansell, London and Wisbech

PREFACE

The present guide is based on the *Short Guide to the Sculptures of the Parthenon* (last impression, 1961) by Bernard Ashmole, Keeper of Greek and Roman Antiquities from 1938 to 1956. The installation of the sculptures in the new gallery presented to the Museum by the late Lord Duveen has, however, necessitated extensive changes in the practical directions given in the text; and at the same time the opportunity has been taken to expand the introductory sections so as to give a rather fuller account of the circumstances in which Lord Elgin acquired the sculptures, as well as of their subsequent history in this country. A substantial increase has also been made in the number of illustrations; and it is hoped that the guide as a whole will serve to commemorate both the opening of the new gallery and the devoted work of all those who in the past have helped to preserve the sculptures for the world.

D. E. L. HAYNES

CONTENTS

I. HISTORY OF THE SCULPTURES

The building of the Parthenon

The temple on the Acropolis known as the Parthenon (the name first occurs in an inscription of the fourth century B C) was built in the third quarter of the fifth century B C (447–432) when Pericles was leader in Athens.

The Acropolis (*fig 1*) is a rocky hill which rises from the plain like the castle-rocks of Windsor or Edinburgh, and from the earliest times it had been both a fortress and the religious centre of the state. The principal cult was that of the maiden goddess Athena, and a new temple in her honour was being constructed on the Acropolis when the Persians invaded Greece in 480 B C. The Persians burnt it, and for a generation the area lay desolate as a memorial of barbarian savagery. In the middle of the fifth century B C Athens had reached a high degree of prosperity. She was receiving and treasuring the tribute paid by the allied states of the Delian Confederacy, and in return provided for their naval defence. Pericles planned to devote the surplus of this tribute to the adornment of the city, although his opponents claimed that it was an improper use of the money, and compared Athens to a 'loose woman bedecking herself with costly jewels'.

fig 2 The explosion of 1687 (after F. Fanelli, *Atene Attica*, 1707)

In his plans the shrine of the patron goddess naturally took first place. The new temple, which had to provide not only a setting for a colossal statue of the goddess, but also a strong-room for the funds of the Confederacy, was built on an extension of the foundations that had belonged to the unfinished temple mentioned above. Ictinus is named as the principal architect, with Callicrates as the second architect, or possibly the contractor. The sculptor Pheidias exercised a general supervision over all the building schemes of Pericles, and was also the creator of the new statue of Athena – the Parthenos – of gold and ivory, which stood inside the temple. This statue, about 40 feet high, was dedicated in 438 BC, which suggests that the building was by then substantially complete.

6

Fragments of the building-accounts, inscribed on marble, have been found in Athens, and dates for the different stages in the construction of the Parthenon and the carving of its sculptures have been inferred from them. This series of accounts ends in 432 BC, the fifteenth year of the work, and it is generally assumed that the sculptures were by that time virtually completed.

Plutarch, in his *Life of Pericles*, describes the intense activity of the time, and adds that it was a matter of astonishment that works of such excellence and importance could be completed within the limits of one administration. Writing five hundred years after the building was erected, he observes that 'every work of the time of Pericles had from the moment of its creation the beauty of an old master, but yet it retains its freshness and newness to this day. There is a certain novelty that seems to bloom upon them, which ever keeps their beauty untouched by time; as if they had perpetual breath of life, and an unaging soul mingled in their composition'.

Later history of the Parthenon

The Parthenon was finished in 432 BC. For the next nine centuries it continued to be a temple of Athena. It then became a Christian Church, dedicated to the Panagia, or Virgin Mary: an apse was made at the East end, and this displaced much of the sculpture there. It so continued for another thousand years, from about AD 450 to AD 1458. In the latter year Athens was taken by the Turks, and not long afterwards, this, its cathedral church, was converted into a Mohammedan mosque. In this condition the building remained, not much damaged, for two centuries more.

In 1674, the Marquis de Nointel, French Ambassador to Turkey, visited Athens. He was accompanied by a draughtsman, probably Jacques Carrey of Troyes, who spent about a fortnight making drawings of architectural and sculptural remains, principally the sculptures of the Parthenon. Carrey made no attempt to reproduce the styles or special beauties of the sculptures, and owing to the speed at which he was obliged to work and to unfavourable conditions, omitted much; but he seldom misinterpreted what was there, or inserted any non-existent detail. His drawings (two of which are reproduced in figures 17 and 22) are preserved in the Bibliothèque Nationale in Paris. They form an invaluable record, for in 1687 a Turkish garrison on the Acropolis was besieged by an army commanded by the Venetian General Francesco Morosini, and in the evening of 26th September one of the besiegers' shells fell on the

fig 3 The Parthenon in 1766 (from a drawing by W. Pars, in the British Museum)

Turkish powder-store, which had been placed in the Parthenon.

A great explosion followed, the interior was destroyed, and the middles of the long sides were blown outwards (*fig 2*). Further grave damage was done by Morosini, who made an unsuccessful attempt to lower the central figures of the west pediment, which had so far remained almost complete. From that time onwards the temple was a ruin; a small and mean mosque was built askew on a part of its floor, and Turkish houses and courtyards encumbered its surroundings (*fig 3*). Its remaining sculptures were continually exposed to the vandalism of stone-robbers, lime-burners, curio-hunters and religious iconoclasts; and, but for the intervention of Lord Elgin in 1800, it is probable that many of them would have perished or been damaged beyond recognition.

Lord Elgin and the Parthenon

Thomas Bruce, seventh earl of Elgin and eleventh earl of Kincardine (*fig 4*), was born on 20th July 1766, and succeeded to the title in 1771, shortly before his fifth birthday. Educated at Harrow and Westminster, St. Andrews and Paris, he entered the diplomatic service in 1790, when he was sent to Brussels on a special mission. In 1792 he was appointed Envoy at Brussels; in 1795 Envoy Extraordinary at Berlin; and in 1799 Ambassador at Constantinople.

Encouraged by his Scottish architect, Thomas Harrison, Elgin resolved that his term of office in Constantinople should be of service to the Arts, and began by sounding his friends in the Government on a proposal for making drawings and casts of the monuments of Athens at public expense. The proposal fell on stony ground in Whitehall; but, undeterred by this disappointment, he determined to carry out his project with his own resources.

Before leaving England he appointed as his private secretary William Richard Hamilton[1], to whose untiring efforts much of his later success was due. He also attempted to assemble a team of artists and architects in this country, approaching, among others, the twenty-four-year-old painter J. M. W. Turner; but he could find nobody prepared to work for him on terms he could afford, and decided to postpone the recruitment until he reached Sicily. Here he was able to secure the services of Giovanni Battista Lusieri, a Neapolitan topographical painter of some distinction, who agreed to take charge of the forthcoming operations at a salary of £200 a year and his keep. Shortly afterwards Hamilton was despatched to Rome, where he engaged a Tartar figure painter, Feodor Ivanovitch ('Lord Elgin's Calmuck'); the architects, Vincenzo Balestra and Sebastian Ittar; and the moulders, Bernardino Ledus and Vincenzo Rosati.

The party of artists reached Athens in July 1800, having called on the way at Constantinople, where Elgin had already taken up his duties. Athens at that date was a small and squalid town, lacking every comfort; and the party's difficulties were greatly increased by the obstruction of the local Turkish authorities, particularly of the Disdar or military commandant, and by the general odium attaching to Christian infidels. The chief monuments on which they were to work – the Parthenon, the Erechtheum, the Temple of Athena Nike (Victory), and the Propylaea – all lay on the Acropolis, to which they were only admitted on payment of the exorbitant sum of five guineas

[1] Later British Minister at Naples (1822-5); not to be confused with his more famous namesake, Sir William Hamilton, who held the same office from 1764 to 1800.

9

fig 4 Lord Elgin, about 1795 (from a drawing by G. P. Harding after Anton Graff, in the British Museum)

a day. Nor, having gained admittance at this price, were they allowed to do more than make drawings, for it was feared that if they were allowed to build scaffolds to take casts, they would be able to over-look the gardens of the surrounding Turkish houses, thereby inhibit-ing the Turkish womenfolk from taking the air. Early in 1801 Lusieri visited Constantinople to report to Elgin and impress on him the necessity for a *firman* or authority from the Turkish government for their operations. Elgin secured the required document without difficulty and despatched it to Athens ahead of Lusieri; but it never reached its destination and when Lusieri returned to his post in April, he found that the Disdar had stopped all work on the Acropo-lis, even drawing. And such was still the situation when in May Philip Hunt, the Embassy Chaplain at Constantinople, arrived to take stock of it on Elgin's behalf.

Hunt saw at once that a new *firman* was indispensable, and he also decided to urge Elgin to make an important change in his plans. Hitherto Elgin had had no intention of removing any sculptures or architectural elements, his sole purpose being to draw, measure and mould. But Hunt, having seen with his own eyes the alarming rate at which the surviving antiquities were being destroyed or otherwise disappearing, drew up a memorandum after his return, in which he recommended Elgin to apply for a *firman* which would not only allow him to achieve his original aims, but also procure him 'liberty to take away any sculptures or inscriptions which do not interfere with the works or walls of the Citadel', this being, in Hunt's view, the only hope of preserving them for posterity. Convinced by Hunt's argu-ments, which no doubt reinforced his own inclinations, Elgin entered into negotiations with the Sublime Porte.

The negotiations were short and fruitful. Recent British successes in the Napoleonic War, especially the expulsion of the French from Egypt which the Turks hoped to regain, had predisposed the Porte to be accommodating to the British Ambassador; and before the middle of July Elgin had the desired *firman* safely in his hands. Addressed to the Voivode and Cadi, the chief civil and religious authorities of Athens, its concluding and operative paragraph is sufficiently interesting to quote:

It is our desire that on the arrival of this letter you use your diligence to act conformably to the instances of the said Ambassador, as long as the said five Artists dwelling at Athens shall be employed in going in and out of the said citadel of Athens, which is the place of their occupations; or in fixing scaffolding around the ancient Temple of the Idols, or in modelling with chalk or gypsum the said ornaments and visible figures thereon; or in measuring the fragments and vestiges of other ruined edifices; or in excavating, when they find it necessary, the foundations, in search of inscriptions among the rubbish; that they be not molested by the said Disdar, nor by any other persons, nor even by you; and that no one meddle with their scaffolding or implements, nor hinder them from taking away any pieces of stone with inscriptions or figures . . .

(Signed) *Seged Abdullah Kaimacan*

Brought to Athens by Hunt himself, the *firman* was delivered to the Voivode on 23rd July and transformed the situation overnight. From now on Lusieri and his artists were allowed to work in the Acropolis without hindrance. While the artists carried on with their recording and moulding, Lusieri threw himself with enthusiasm into the task of collecting sculptures.

His activities on the Acropolis lasted from July 1801 until the beginning of 1804. During this period Elgin himself was only once able to visit Athens: in April 1802, at the beginning of a four-months' tour of Greece, in which he had not previously set foot. Hunt and Hamilton also made occasional appearances, but for most of the time Lusieri was left to his own devices. Many of the sculptures of the Parthenon which he collected were found buried in the ground where they had fallen from the building; others were retrieved from later structures into which they had been built; but the majority were taken down from the building itself. The work of removal was carried out by Lusieri with great care, and only one accident, involving minor damage to the architecture, is recorded. By the beginning of 1804 Lusieri had possessed himself of all the sculpture he could without endangering the fabric of the building. Of the original 524 feet of the frieze, 247 had been taken; of the 92 metopes, 14; of the pedimental figures, 17. At the same time he had made other important acquisitions on Elgin's behalf, including a Caryatid and column from the Erechtheum, four slabs of the frieze of the Temple of Victory, the statue of Dionysus from the monument of Thrasyllus; a number of Greek reliefs, and fragments from Mycenae. Meanwhile, the other artists, having finished all they could usefully do, had been dismissed in the spring of 1803. The *formatori* had by then moulded the whole of the West frieze of the Parthenon, parts of the North frieze, and six of the metopes, as well as the frieze and three metopes of the Hephaesteum and the frieze of the monument of Lysicrates.

As the sculptures and moulds accumulated, ways and means had to be found to ship them back to England. The first consignment was despatched to Alexandria in December 1801 in a Ragusan brig; and a second followed in January 1802 in the *Mentor*, a brig purchased by Elgin for the purpose. On her next voyage, however, the *Mentor* met with disaster. Sailing from Peiraeus on 15th September, she was wrecked off Cerigo (Cythera) two days later, and seventeen cases of sculpture went to the bottom. Fortunately all were eventually recovered by divers and forwarded, through the good offices of Lord Nelson, to Malta; but the salvage took four years and the whole episode cost Elgin £5000. In the meantime every opportunity had been taken to embark further consignments, most of them being taken to Malta and there trans-shipped; and by January 1804, the greater part of the collection was already safely in England. But there were still forty cases awaiting shipment in Peiraeus when England declared war on Turkey in February 1807. Sequestrated at the beginning of the war, the cases were not released until long after its end in January 1809; and another two years had passed before their contents were finally reunited with the marbles in England.

The Reception of the Marbles in England and Purchase Negotiations

In January 1803, his term of office in Constantinople having expired, Elgin set out for home. In Rome, where he spent Easter, he took the opportunity of consulting Canova on the question of restoring the marbles. Although he had not yet seen them, Canova's reply was unequivocal: 'it would be sacrilege in him or any man to touch them with a chisel'. From Italy Elgin continued his journey through France, where he had the misfortune to be caught by the decree of *2 Prairial* ordaining the detention of all Englishmen between eighteen and sixty as prisoners of war. He was arrested in Paris about 23rd May and remained in France as a prisoner until the summer of 1806, when he was allowed to return to England on parole.

The cases of sculpture which had already arrived in England before his release had been stored unopened in Privy Gardens, Whitehall, first at the Duchess of Portland's house, later at the Duke of Richmond's. Shortly after his return, Elgin had them transferred to a house he had leased at the corner of Park Lane and Piccadilly, where the sculptures were installed in a large shed built in the grounds to receive them. From the summer of 1807, the installation being completed, permission was given to selected visitors to view the marbles, and among those admitted were the artists Flaxman, Wilkie, Haydon, Fuseli, West and Lawrence. All were deeply impressed by what they saw, particularly Haydon who was enthusiastic in his praise: 'I felt as if a divine truth had blazed inwardly upon my mind, and I knew that they (the marbles) would at last rouse the art of Europe from its slumber of darkness.' Another visitor to Park Lane was the famous actress Mrs Siddons who, in the opinion of Lawrence, could 'nowhere be seen with so just accompaniments as the works of Pheidias, nor can they receive nobler homage than from her praise'.

The shed at Park Lane was never intended by Elgin as more than a temporary expedient; but the difficulty of providing more permanent and suitable accommodation for the marbles out of his own depleted resources was such that by the beginning of 1810 he was seriously considering the possibility of offering his collection to the nation. The universal admiration which the marbles had already won encouraged him to believe that the government would be favourably disposed towards their purchase, and this hope was presently fortified by direct overtures from Mr Planta, the Principal Librarian of the British Museum. On 3rd May 1811, after a year of informal negotiation, Elgin wrote to the Paymaster-General offering his collection to the nation for £62,440, a sum composed of his disbursements for its acquisition and fourteen years' interest. The government's response was a bitter disappointment; no formal reply was made to Elgin's offer, but it was unofficially intimated to him that the most the Government would be prepared to pay was £30,000.

Meanwhile the house at Park Lane had been sold, and the removal of the marbles was urgent. After a vain attempt to lend them to the British Institution, Elgin approached the Duke of Devonshire, who agreed to allow him limited tenure of a shed in the yard of Burlington House; and hither, in the summer of 1811, the marbles were transferred. A year later their numbers were substantially increased by the arrival of those which had been delayed by sequestration in Greece. Among the visitors who saw the collection at Burlington House were Visconti, the most celebrated archaeologist of the day, and Canova. Visconti, who had been invited to London at Elgin's expense, later produced a laudatory memoir; but more impressive, because disinterested, is the tribute of Canova: 'Oh that I had but to begin again! to unlearn all that I had learned – I now at last see what ought to form the real school of sculpture.'

Visconti's opinion of the marbles had been solicited by Elgin as ammunition for further negotiations with the Government, which had hardly begun when, in March 1815, he learnt to his dismay that Burlington House had been sold and was about to be rebuilt. A warning that the rebuilding would start in a fortnight was fortunately premature; but it was clear that an early decision on the future of the marbles was imperative; and on 8th June, having talked the whole matter over with Hamilton, he wrote to the Chancellor of the

Exchequer, again offering his collection to the nation, but at a revised figure of £73,600; in the event of this offer being refused, he requested that the value of the collection should be determined by a special Committee of the House of Commons, by whose assessment he declared himself ready to abide. The Chancellor in his reply discreetly ignored the offer, but welcomed the idea of a committee and suggested, as a possible procedure, that Elgin should himself submit a suitable petition to Parliament. A petition was accordingly presented to the House on Elgin's behalf on 15th June; but in view of the many questions it provoked, not to mention the supervening excitements of Waterloo, further consideration of the matter was postponed to the next session. In consequence, a second petition in the same terms, but supported now by a recommendation from the Prince Regent, was presented by the Chancellor of the Exchequer on 15th February of the following year. A debate followed on the 23rd, and after some discussion the appointment of a Select Committee was approved.

The Committee sat on eight days between 29th February and 13th March, and reported on 25th March. It had considered Elgin's petition under four heads:

1 The authority by which the collection was acquired;
2 The circumstances under which that authority was granted;
3 The merit of the marbles as works of sculpture, and the importance of making them public property, for the purpose of promoting the study of the Fine Arts in Great Britain;
4 Their value as objects of sale; which included consideration of the expense which had attended the removing, transporting, and bringing them to England.

Under the first head the Committee found that Elgin had full authority from the Turkish Government for his activities; under the second, that he had acted in a private capacity, though only an Ambassador would have obtained such extensive powers. Under the third head the Committee was able to report that the eminent artists it had examined (they were Nollekens, Flaxman, Westmacott, Chantrey, Rossi, Lawrence, Wilkins and West) concurred in rating the marbles 'in the very first class of ancient art, some placing them a little above, and others but very little below the Apollo Belvidere, the Laocoon, and the Torso of the Belvidere'. The only dissentient opinion expressed was that of Richard Payne Knight, a member of the Society of Dilettanti, who had already done his best to prejudice Elgin's case in the preceding negotiations by reviving a fanciful theory of the seventeenth-century French traveller, Spon, that several of the pedimental figures were replacements of the time of the Roman emperor Hadrian. It is much to the Committee's credit that it discounted Payne Knight's pompous bigotry. As to the value, the Committee concluded that £35,000 (a figure suggested by Lord Aberdeen in evidence) would be a reasonable and sufficient price; and added a recommendation that Elgin, and his heirs being Earls of Elgin, should be added to the Trustees of the British Museum.

Elgin was deeply disappointed by the Committee's valuation, and found the Report as a whole pervaded by 'manifest coldness and ill-will'; but there was nothing more he could do. On 7th June the Report was debated in the House and adopted by eighty-two votes to thirty.

The Marbles in the British Museum

The transfer of the marbles from Burlington House to the Museum began at once, and at the same time a temporary gallery was built in the Museum grounds for their reception. The gallery, a view of which is given in the painting by A. Archer reproduced as a frontispiece to this book, was opened to the public in January, 1817, and served for fourteen years, being dismantled in 1831 to make way for a permanent gallery erected as part of the general rebuilding programme. Known successively as the Elgin Room, the Second Elgin Room, and the Large Elgin Room, this new gallery continued to house the main body of the sculptures until 1961, but in 1857 the pedimental figures were removed to the newly-built 'First Elgin Room' (the present Ephesus Room) where they remained until 1869 In that year the whole collection was reunited in the Second Elgin Room, which had now been enlarged by a northward extension (walled off in 1939 and known as the 'Small Elgin Room' after 1949).

The arrangement of the sculptures adopted in 1869 remained substantially unchanged until 1939. The pedimental figures were taken down to the basement for safety in 1915, but replaced in their old positions on the reopening of the gallery in 1919. By now, however, as a result of the general change of ideas on museum display, the arrangement had begun to attract widespread criticism. Its guiding principle had been to present the sculptural decoration of the Parthenon in as complete a form as possible, and for that reason the marbles were supplemented by an extensive series of plaster-casts of pieces not in England and interspersed with models and other illustrative material. Valuable as this comprehensive exhibition was for the archaeologist, it tended to leave the ordinary visitor confused, and unable to distinguish one material from the other. Moreover, in the limited space available, it inevitably resulted in an unpleasant congestion and interference of one part of the display with another. In 1928 these criticisms found public expression in a report of the Royal Commission on National Museums and Galleries and at once elicited a generous offer from Sir Joseph (later Lord) Duveen to build a new gallery for the sculptures of the Parthenon at his own expense.

fig 5 The Duveen Gallery (*photograph*, James Mortimer)

The offer was gratefully accepted by the Trustees, and in 1930 John Russell Pope, a New York architect, was invited to draw up preliminary plans. Discussion of the plans was protracted and it was not until 1936 that the work, which was estimated to cost £100,000, was put in hand. The gallery was completed in 1938, and an opening ceremony was planned for the following summer; but while the sculptures were still being transferred to their new positions, it became clear that war was imminent. In expectation of immediate air-raids the sculptures were hurriedly assembled in the transepts, deemed the strongest parts of the gallery, and there protected by lean-to structures of corrugated iron supported on timber balks and covered by sand-bags. Later the frieze was removed to an unused section of the London Underground Railway, and the pedimental figures and metopes were taken down to the Museum vaults.

The Duveen Gallery was seriously damaged by bombing in 1940, and was still unfit for use when the time came to put the sculptures on exhibition again after the war. To resuscitate the congested pre-war arrangement was, however, out of the question; and it was therefore decided not only to omit the casts, but to increase the former exhibition space by two rooms. The pedimental sculptures and frieze were placed in the Large and Small Elgin Rooms; the metopes in the adjacent room to the north, which before the war had housed the frieze from Bassae; the models and other illustrative material in the former Nereid Room. The rooms were opened in 1949.

Restoration of the Duveen Gallery began in the summer of 1960 and was completed twelve months later, the work having included the valuable but invisible addition of an electrostatic precipitator for cleansing the air. Now that the marbles themselves have found a worthy home in the new gallery (*fig 5*), it is hoped that it will not be long before justice can be done to the banished casts – a collection unique in its importance and comprehensiveness – by exhibiting them in the basement beneath.

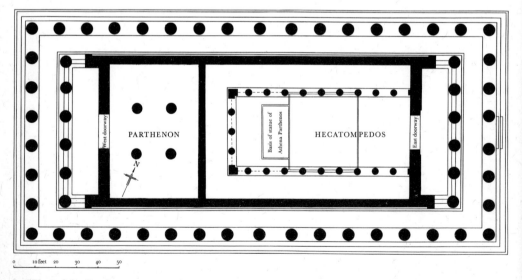

fig 6 Plan of the Parthenon

II. THE ARCHITECTURE OF THE PARTHENON AND THE POSITION OF THE SCULPTURES ON THE BUILDING

The Parthenon (*figs 6–8*) was an oblong building, with a porch formed of six columns, at each end: round this kernel ran an outer row of columns, forty-six in all (eight at each end and seventeen on each flank, if we count the corner columns twice); and a roof of low pitch covered the whole structure. The temple is of the Doric order and built throughout of marble quarried on Mount Pentelicus, ten miles from Athens: the columns, which are stout with broad shallow flutes, support a plain marble beam known as the epistyle (architrave) and above the epistyle a series of panels, each about 4 feet square, sculptured in high relief–the METOPES–alternating with sets of vertical bands and grooves known as triglyphs. Above this, at each end of the building, is a low triangle formed by the pitch of the roof, called by the Greeks aetos ('eagle'), in English PEDIMENT (a word of which the derivation is obscure): it was nearly 100 feet long,

fig 7 The Parthenon from the west

19

over 11 feet high in the centre, and was filled by a series of sculptures which are virtually statues in the round, except that none could be more than 3 feet from front to back owing to the shallow space. The temple proper consists of two chambers back to back without inter-

PEDIMENT

METOPES

FRIEZE

fig 8 Sectional diagram of the Parthenon, showing the position of the sculptures (after G. Niemann)

communication: that facing east contained the cult-statue, whilst the smaller, facing west, was a treasury. A FRIEZE (just over 3 feet high and originally half that in thickness), sculptured in low relief, ran round the top of the outer wall of these chambers and continued above the columns of the porches at each end.

There are thus three kinds of sculptured decoration, all of Pentelic marble: the FRIEZE, the PEDIMENTS, and the METOPES. The metopes were made first, probably not before 447 BC: the pediments last, probably 438–432 BC, and the frieze some time in between, probably in the years round 440 BC. Figure 8 shows clearly the position of each kind of sculpture on the building. Both architecture and sculpture were coloured, and this colour served to throw the carving into bolder relief, but much of the fine detail which can now be seen must have been completely lost owing to the distance from the ground at which the sculptures were set. The frieze, too, was awkwardly placed: both angle of view and lighting were peculiar. It was masked by the upper part of the outer colonnade until the spectator was close underneath the building. Light could strike up from below on to the frieze or be diffused from surrounding architectural members, but there was no light, except reflected light, from above. The sculptor who designed it attempted to mitigate the effect of the steep angle of view by arranging that the upper part should be in higher relief than the lower: at the top the projection is sometimes as much as $2\frac{1}{4}$ inches, diminishing towards the bottom, where it seldom exceeds $1\frac{1}{4}$ inches, and is often lower. The background is kept vertical, so that in effect the figures are leaning outwards from the top.

III. GUIDE TO THE EXHIBITION

For plan see inside front cover

South Slip Room

The visitor is recommended, before entering the main exhibition, to study the material illustrating the structure, sculptures and history of the Parthenon collected in the South Slip Room on the left of the vestibule of the Duveen Gallery.

The Main Gallery

This room contains the frieze of the Parthenon.

Before the frieze is examined in detail, a word should be said on its subject. It is evident that the greater part represents some festal and ceremonial procession in which many parts of the community take a share. In ancient Athens the most important of such processions was that which formed the central event of the Panathenaic festival. This was celebrated every year, but it recurred every four years with especial splendour under the name of the Great Panathenaea. Clearly, on the frieze of the Parthenon we have an idealized rendering of the procession at the Great Panathenaea.

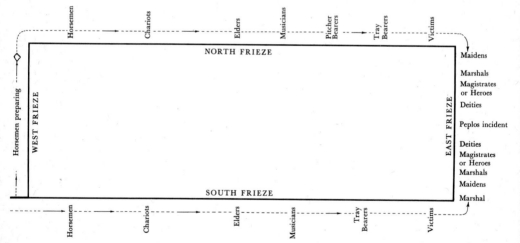

fig 9 Plan of the frieze, showing the order of the Panathenaic procession

The prime motive of the procession was to form an escort from the lower town to the Acropolis for a sacred robe (the peplos), which was woven afresh every four years for the purpose of draping the primitive wooden image of Athena in another temple on the Acropolis. The diagram (*fig 9*) explains how the various parts of the procession and the ceremony are arranged on the frieze. We see the ceremonial folding of the robe in the centre of the East end: the event is spiritualized by being made to take place in the presence of a company of twelve gods, who are seen enthroned as guests and spectators. Beyond the gods on right and left are two companies of citizens, and two troops of maidens coming up from either side at the head of the two branches of the procession. These two branches have each started at the South-west corner of the building but move in opposite directions. Upon the two long sides of the temple – North and South – they form parallel and similarly composed streams, flowing from west to east, that on the North side thus moving from right to left, that on the South from left to right. Each, before it turns the corner on to the East front, is headed by the animals for sacrifice with their attendant escorts. These are followed by bearers of other sacrificial offerings, by musicians, elders, chariots, and lastly by the splendid prancing tumult of the riders.

fig 10 West Frieze, slab VIII (Lord Elgin's cast)

The West side was not divided in the centre, like the East side, but the movement on it was northwards (from right to left) so that it linked up with the rear of the procession on the North side.

The original length of the frieze was 524 feet, of which 247 feet are in the British Museum; 176 feet exist elsewhere; 56 feet are recorded in old drawings; and about 45 feet are altogether lost.

In the Museum, each slab of the frieze has its number in Roman numerals, and each person represented on the frieze has his or her number in Arabic numerals. These numbers are consecutive, except occasionally where an earlier placing of the slab has been found to be incorrect and has been altered, but the numbering has been retained to avoid confusion.

THE
WEST
FRIEZE

Immediately to the right of the visitor as he enters the Main Gallery are slabs II and I of the West Frieze (slab II is marked ◇ in fig 9 and on plan inside front cover). The remainder of the West Frieze is still in position on the building but photographs of the casts taken by Lord Elgin in 1802, which are of unique importance since they reproduce details which have since perished, are exhibited in the South Slip Room. Lord Elgin's cast of slab VIII is shown on figure 10.

The West Frieze, which was probably the first to be carved, shows horsemen, with their attendants, preparing themselves and their horses to take part in the Panathenaic procession: some are adjusting harness, fastening clothing and boots, others mounting their horses and starting to move off. As the procession, which started at the

fig 11 West Frieze, slab II (*photograph*, James Mortimer)

South-west corner, approaches the North-west corner, it gathers speed, and the two leading horsemen (2, 3) who appear on this last slab are already at a canter (*fig. 11*). The last figure of the West

Frieze (1), who is actually carved on the return end of the block which forms the first slab of the North Frieze, is one of the officials who was charged with marshalling the procession. His quiet stance and simple drapery give stability to the design at the corner-stone of the building.

Continuing along this side of the gallery, we pass the North-West angle of the frieze and come to the first slab of the North Frieze.

This begins, as appropriate at the angle of the building, with quiet scenes, a boy arranging his master's tunic before he mounts (134, 133), and a horseman (131) holding his horse with one hand and adjusting his wreath with the other (slab XLII, *fig 12*).

fig 12 North Frieze, slab XLII (*photograph*, James Mortimer)

From this point the procession moves forward at a trot, now breaking into a canter, now checking, and the number of horsemen taking part in it increases until (although the height of the relief nowhere exceeds $2\frac{1}{4}$ inches) groups of five, six, and sometimes no fewer than seven, are shown as riding nearly abreast (*fig 13*). The nearest horseman of each group can usually be distinguished as an isolated figure sometimes turning towards us (e.g. 129, 111). The general effect of a prancing troop of spirited horses, held well in check by riders with a nice hand and easy seat, is admirably rendered. The effect of depth in space is achieved by a successive series

25

fig 13 North Frieze slab XXXVIII (*photograph*, James Mortimer)

of overlapping surfaces forming wave upon wave of relief, and the outlines of the complex design are kept distinct by sharp cutting inwards from the flat front plane of the marble. Originally the coloured background, showing above and below the riders, served to throw the figures into bold silhouette. The reins and bridles, when not indicated by painting, were of bronze, and rivet-holes for their attachment can often be seen behind the horse's ear, at his mouth, and in the rider's hands: stirrups were unknown in antiquity.

The leading horsemen of the cavalcade are those on slab XXIV, *which is the last slab on this wall; the remainder of the North Frieze is on the opposite wall.*

On the left of the slab XXIV may be seen the inside of the rim of a shield and an arm holding it. This shows us that we have now reached the chariots in the procession, for each chariot carried not only a charioteer but an armed man, who showed his agility and skill by leaping on and off the chariot whilst it was in motion; and it is to one of these that the shield and arm belong. The chariots are four-horsed, and the charioteers, who are all men, wear the long robe which was

26

their customary dress. The first chariot is standing still (slab XXIII). Others in front of it are in motion, often rapid motion, and they are checked by marshals (e.g. 59, 45) to prevent them overrunning those who precede them on foot. The next part of the frieze suffered severely in the explosion of 1687, and can be made out only with difficulty. Much of it was intact in Carrey's time (1674), and two or three fine slabs are preserved in Athens, having been flung from the building and buried by the explosion. With the help of these and of the drawings by Carrey and by Stuart (1752) it is possible to determine how the procession was made up: in front of the chariots came a group of old men; these were probably the branch-bearers (*thallophori*), elderly citizens who carried olive branches; they were preceded by four lyre-players and four flute-players, and they in turn by four boys carrying water-pots containing water for ritual use. Three boys bearing trays of offerings, one of whom survives (13), headed this part of the procession. In front of them were sacrificial victims—sheep and heifers—with their attendants, the leading heifer being on the most easterly slab of the frieze.

The East Frieze (fig 14) occupies all the space between the two doors in this wall; and two slabs (VI and VIII) are on the right of the North door. It is helpful in understanding the subject and design to stand some distance away from the frieze opposite the central scene (slab V). **THE EAST FRIEZE**

The left part is more complete, and helps us to reconstruct the right, for the two branches of the procession which started at the South-west corner of the building, and which are now converging on the East front, are similar to each other in their main features. The leading groups in each are no longer men but girls, carrying various vessels for use in the sacrifices. Nos. 56 and 57, for instance, carry between them a tall incense-burner, nos. 58 and 59 and nos. 7–11, jugs; others hold phialae—shallow bowls for pouring libations. Nos. 12–15 carry two objects whose use is uncertain; they look like stands with spreading bases, and it has been suggested that they are 'dogs' for the spits on which the sacrifices would be roasted; or they may have been used somehow in connexion with the peplos, the sacred robe for the goddess. It is noteworthy that the girls at the head of each branch of the procession (e.g. 16, 17) carry nothing at all: almost certainly they are those who had been bearing the peplos which is now in the hands of the priest (on slab V); and it is possible that they are also the *arrephori*, the maidens who had charge of the weaving of the robe. The four maidens leading the procession on the

fig 14 East Frieze, slabs IV–VI

right are being received by two men, evidently officials; another man stands waiting[1], whilst a fourth beckons across to the left as if to the other half of the procession. To the left is a group of four men (43–6) standing in easy attitudes conversing or looking at the approaching procession: they have been thought to be magistrates, representative citizens, or perhaps heroic ancestors of the Athenians. Their heads, hacked off by the Turks about 1795, are lost; but casts, made by a Frenchman just before, have survived. They balance a similar but not identical group on the left at an equal distance away from the central slab; the first figure on the left of this latter group (20) has sometimes been thought to be Pericles. We now look back to the central slab itself. This is a magnificent block of marble, 14 feet 6 inches long, which was set over the columns in front of the main Eastern doorway of the temple. On it the climax of the whole ceremony is represented: a priest (34), aided by a young boy, is holding the peplos which has been woven for presentation to the goddess, whilst the priestess of Athena (33) is about to lift down one of two stools which are being brought by her attendants (31–2), as a symbolic invitation to the gods to be present on this sacred occasion ('Theoxenia'). It will be seen that on each side of this central scene is a group of seated figures on a larger scale than any others on the frieze. They are twelve in all, with two younger ones, and there is no doubt that they are the twelve gods of Olympus imagined as invisible spectators of the ceremony. The identifications of these deities are established by a careful study of their positions in relation to the central scene, by their gestures, by their appearance and their dress, and by the objects which they once held: these were sometimes made separately in bronze and fastened into small drill-holes which still remain, sometimes indicated by painting.

The most northerly pair of these seated figures, those on our right, are fragmentary, but their identification is certain: the boy Eros, god of love, holding a parasol to protect his mother Aphrodite from the sun, survives only in a cast made about 1790: the marble was broken up soon after, and the figure of Aphrodite almost entirely destroyed.

Next come Artemis, her brother Apollo, and Poseidon, god of the sea, on a well-preserved slab in Athens. Poseidon's trident, of which his left hand held the shaft, was shown in paint on the background. We now come to the slab next the central scene, and this evidently should contain deities closely associated with Athens. The first (37) is a god of powerful physique and stocky build: he can be no other than HEPHAESTUS, god of crafts, who was a close associate of

[1] This slab is in the Louvre.

Athena at Athens, and shared a temple with her (the so-called 'Theseion') in the craftsmen's quarter. According to legend he was lame, and this is suggested in the sculpture by the stick with which he supports his right arm-pit, and by the thickness of his right ankle. He was turning his head to speak to the companion on his left (36), a goddess whose position next to the central scene must be significant. She sits close to the peplos and is, in fact, ATHENA herself, who, since this is a peaceful occasion, has removed not only her helmet, but her warlike aegis (a narrow leather breastplate covered with metal scales, and bearing the gorgon's head) which she holds on her lap under her left hand. Her right hand originally held a spear; it was of bronze, and three drill-holes, in a line, show where it was attached. The position on the left of the central scene, corresponding to that of Athena on the right, must obviously be occupied by a deity of great importance (30). He is ZEUS, supreme among the gods, and father of Athena: whereas the others sit on stools, he has a throne with a back, and a side-rail supported at its front end by a sphinx (still just discernible): in his right hand he holds the shaft of a sceptre, the lower end of which was of bronze. The goddess seated in front of him (29) is his consort HERA, who turns towards him and holds back her veil—then, as now, a symbol of the bride: she is wearing a wreath of serrated leaves, perhaps willow, a tree sacred to her in her great sanctuary on the island of Samos. To the left of Hera stands a young girl with wings (28), who holds her left hand to her hair and her right to her girdle as if fastening them in place after alighting. She may be NIKE (Victory), or IRIS, messenger of the gods. Nike is the attendant of Zeus, Iris perhaps more closely associated with Hera, and either identification is possible. (The head of this figure, beautifully preserved, is in Athens, having been broken off in very early times and built into a Byzantine wall on the Acropolis, where it was discovered in 1889. The way in which the faces of all the other figures just described have been, not weathered, but deliberately chipped away, is an example of the fate of those sculptures which remained exposed.)

On the left of this last figure is a god seated in a restless attitude (27), he has drawn up his right knee and is clasping it with his hands. He is ARES, the god of war, uneasy at this peaceful ceremony: the shaft of his spear (part sculptured, the rest painted) passes behind, and supports, his left heel. In front of Ares sits a matronly goddess (26), heavily draped, chin in hand—in antiquity a gesture of sadness: in her left hand she holds a long torch which originally continued upwards to the right: its upper end is broken away in front of the face of Ares. This is no doubt DEMETER, goddess of the grain-bearing earth, whose sorrowing search for her daughter Persephone, carried off by Hades to the underworld, was familiar not only in legend but from its enactment at the Eleusinian Mysteries. A god sits opposite Demeter, with his knees touching hers (25): this must be DIONYSUS, the other great god of fertility, giver of the grape as she is of the grain; his left hand once held the shaft of his thyrsus, a wand capped with a bunch of ivy (this was depicted in paint); and his character is shown by his use of a cushion to sit on: he leans back in a friendly fashion on the shoulder of HERMES, herald and messenger of the gods (24): Hermes, in legend, is closely associated with Dionysus, whom he carried when newly born to be nursed by the Nymphs on Mount Nysa. He sits, appropriately, at one end of the group, and faces outwards, ready to move at a moment's notice; he is easily identified by his cloak, boots, and the broad-brimmed hat on his knee (all traveller's gear), and by the herald's staff of bronze once held in his right hand.

fig 15 South Frieze, slab XXX (*photograph*, James Mortimer)

We have already discussed (pages 27 and 30) the figures who stand to the left of the group of gods – the marshals (18, 19), the magistrates (20–23), and the maidens carrying sacrificial vessels; we meet and pass these, and (on the far side of the South doorway) arrive at the first figure of the East Frieze (1), who is carved on the return of the last slab of the South Frieze. He is a marshal who was looking back and beckoning to the procession on the South, thus linking the East and South sides.

fig 16 South Frieze, slab XL

At this point the visitor may either follow along this wall against the flow of the southern branch of the procession or cross to the entrance of the Main Gallery and follow its movement from the beginning (slab I).

THE
SOUTH
FRIEZE

This branch of the procession is made up much as the other was, except that the sacrificial victims consist only of heifers instead of the sheep and heifers of the North. The South Frieze is rather more uneven in quality than the others, but at its best is not surpassed by them: the renderings of cattle (slab XXXVIII) and of galloping horses

33

fig 17 The West Pediment of the Parthenon in 1674 (from a drawing by Jacques
Carrey, in the Bibliothèque Nationale, Paris)

(XXX, *fig 15*) are specially noteworthy. Some of the victims move
quietly (e.g. XXXVIII), one (XL, *fig. 16*) raises its head restively.
There is no doubt that Keats, in his *Ode on a Grecian Urn* (which
combines, poetically, elements from several works of sculpture), had
partly in his mind the frieze of the Parthenon, and possibly this very
slab, when he wrote of 'that heifer lowing at the skies'. Another heifer
(XXXIX) is trying to escape, and its attendant is obliged to throw all
his weight back to check it, placing his foot against a rock as he does
so: the rope on which he is pulling must have been indicated in paint.

The victims were probably followed by bearers of offerings,
musicians, and thallophori (branch-bearers), but the slabs on which
they were represented have been lost or severely damaged, like the
corresponding part of the North Frieze. Chariots follow: at the gallop
(XXX) or almost still (XXV: where the marshal's outstretched arm is
exquisitely modelled); and the chariots in turn are followed by the
troops of horsemen.

The South Transept

We now pass into the South Transept which contains the remains of the West Pediment and Metopes II–IX. The figures of the pediments are not numbered, but lettered.

As the drawing by Carrey (*fig. 17*) shows, the West Pediment was fairly well preserved until the seventeenth century. Its destruction was the work of the Venetian general Morosini, who made a disastrous attempt in 1687 to take down the figure of Poseidon and the horses of the central group. They were shattered when his tackle collapsed, and no effort was made to collect the fragments, which were damaged, and eventually buried, or burnt into lime. The pediment is now represented by little except torsos and a large series of fragments.

THE WEST PEDIMENT

The subjects of the two pediments are briefly mentioned by Pausanias, a traveller who wrote a description of Greece in the second century AD. That of the West Pediment was the CONTEST OF ATHENA AND POSEIDON for the land of Attica, a primitive legend which perhaps echoes some conflict between the deities of two races finally blended to form the population of Athens. The story was that Poseidon in support of his claim struck with his trident the Acropolis rock and produced a miraculous salt-spring: the alleged trident-mark can still be seen, and a salt-spring survived there until at least the second century AD. Athena for her part caused the first olive-tree to appear, and was adjudged the victor: in classical times a sacred olive-tree always grew in a shrine of Athena near the other emblems. The importance in Athenian eyes of the olive, and of the sea, is reflected in this legend.

fig 18 West Pediment, IRIS (*photograph*, James Mortimer)

The designer of the West Pediment of the Parthenon showed the two contestants in the act of producing their portents; the olive-tree probably filled the centre of the pediment. Both ATHENA (L) and POSEIDON (M) have driven up to the contest in two-horse chariots, and have been conducted to it by the two divine messengers, HERMES and IRIS (H, N). The torso of Hermes (H) is much weathered, but that of Iris (N, *fig 18*) is better preserved: she was winged, as the sockets on her shoulders show, and was rushing forwards: the movement, and the modelling of the forms under the thin drapery, make this one of the noblest figures that have survived. The figure in the North (left) angle of the pediment (A, *fig 19*) has suffered less damage than most, owing to the lowness of the roof over it, and it is worthy of long study from every angle. It is usually identified as the god of one of the rivers of Athens, either the CEPHISUS or the ILISSUS: this identification is supported by the flowing character of the drapery and by a statement of Pausanias (the Greek traveller of the second century A D.) that the somewhat similar figures in the angles of the East Pediment of the temple of Zeus at Olympia are river-gods. He has been reclining, and raises himself on his left hand in order to look round at what is going on in the centre. The resulting movement of bones and internal organs, and the tension and relaxation of muscles and skin are rendered in essentials — and in essentials only — with incomparable mastery.

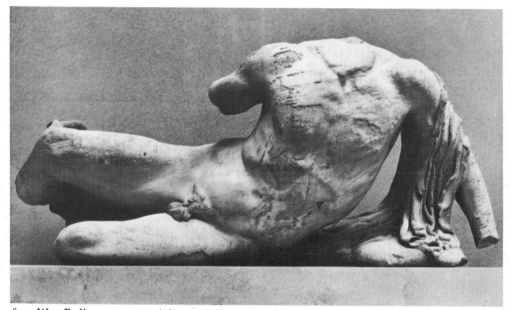

fig 19 West Pediment, ILISSUS (*photograph*, James Mortimer)

The torso (o) to the right of Iris belongs, as may be seen from Carrey's drawing, to the driver of Poseidon's chariot, perhaps Amphitrite his wife: she was leaning backwards to throw her weight on the reins and check the horses. The figure to the right (Q), of which only the lower part survives, may have been a sea-nymph: she was nursing a boy on her knee; her drapery seems soft and wet, and as if ruffled by the breeze.

THE
METOPES

From the construction of the temple the metopes, which are panels keyed into the triglyphs, must be inserted in it at an early stage, and this fact partly accounts for their earlier style and uneven quality. An idea of their architectural framing can be gained from figures 7 and 8. This explains the value of the bold relief in which they are executed: the projection of the sculpture from the background is sometimes as much as 13 inches. Various pieces have been made separately and attached, and there are traces of miscalculations and alterations. There were ninety-two metopes on the Parthenon. The subjects were: on the East, the battle of the gods and the giants; on the West, the battle of the Greeks and the Amazons; on the North and South, scenes from the Trojan legend and from the battle between the Lapiths and the centaurs. All the fifteen in the British Museum belong to the South side, the first eight to the western end of that side (nos. II to IX: no. I is still in position on the building); the last seven (nos. XXVI to XXXII) to its eastern. All represent incidents in the battle between Lapiths and centaurs. The Lapiths were a people living in the mountainous districts of Thessaly, in northern Greece. To the wedding of their king Peirithous were invited their neighbours the centaurs, a tribe so wild that only their upper part was human, the remainder being in the form of a horse. Inflamed with wine, the centaurs attacked the bride and the other women at the feast, but after a violent struggle were defeated. The fight between the Lapiths and centaurs was a favourite subject in Greek art, and typified the struggle between civilization and barbarism.

Eight of the metopes (nos. II–IX) are exhibited in this transept, the series beginning on the left of the entrance. They are numbered in Roman numerals to indicate their position on the building, whilst the British Museum numbers are Arabic. The corners of some of the metopes are made up in plaster, in order to give each scene its square background: these modern parts are lighter in colour.

Metope II. 305. Here the Lapith is kneeling on the centaur's back, gripping him by the beard and forcing him down. Part of the centaur's left hand can be seen: it is trying to relieve the pressure on his throat. The rendering of the tail is curious, as if some flaw in the marble necessitated re-cutting it.

Metope III. 306. Not such a closely joined action as the preceding. The centaur uses a skin as a shield: the Lapith wears boots, and two drill-holes in his body are for the attachment of a bronze sword-belt. Similar holes in the centaur's body may have been for a weapon held in the right hand.

Metope IV. 307. The centaur dashes down a wine-jar from the wedding-feast on his opponent, who is falling backwards and trying to defend himself with a shield. The heads of these two figures are in Copenhagen, having been sent from Athens in 1688 by a Dane serving in Morosini's army.

Metope V. 308. Part of the head of the centaur is in Würzburg. The body of the Lapith, now missing, is shown in a drawing by Carrey: he was trying to hold the centaur at a distance.

Metope VI. 309. An old, fat centaur trying to seize a boy.

This metope has a curious history: it was blown down by a storm from its place on the temple and broken into three, then obtained by a French agent for Choiseul-Gouffier, the French Ambassador to Turkey, in December 1788, but not shipped from Athens till 1802. It was then captured by a British cruiser, and was finally bought out of the custom-house by Lord Elgin, who offered to return it to Choiseul-Gouffier in 1815. The latter took no steps to recover it, and it passed with the Elgin Collection to the British Museum, 'deposited in this collection until M. de Choiseul shall cause it to be removed'.

Metope VII. 310. Vigorous action: the Lapith grapples the centaur's left hand with his left, and draws back his right hand for a blow. The head of the Lapith is in the Louvre, that of the centaur in Athens.

Metope VIII. 311. The Lapith is being forced down on to his heel whilst the centaur was leaning over to dispatch him. The right hind foot of the centaur rests on a rock: the hoof is not carved, and the tail is unfinished. The upper half of the background is restored.

Metope IX. 312. The centaur seizes the Lapith by the left ankle, and rolls him backwards over a wine-jar. The Lapith seizes his antagonist by the hair with his left hand, whilst he was stretching out his right backwards vainly seeking some support. Upper part of background restored. The head of the centaur is in Athens.

At this point there is a gap in the series, the metopes in the middle of the flank of the building having been destroyed by the explosion of 1687: sixteen are missing, though some fragments survive.

We now cross into the North Transept which contains Metopes XXVI–XXXII *and the remains of the East Pediment.*

Metope XXVI. 315. The centaur is rearing up to strike, and the Lapith endeavours to keep him off with hand and foot. The position is so momentary and both antagonists so obviously unable to exert any force that this metope seems weak and unsatisfactory. There has also been some difficulty with the carving: the Lapith's cloak has been chiselled away between arm and thigh, but there are large drill-

fig 20 South Metope XXVII, Lapith and Centaur (*photograph*, James Mortimer)

fig 21 South Metope XXVIII, Lapith and Centaur (*photograph*, James Mortimer)

holes on his left upper arm which may have been to attach an end of the cloak, shown as hanging free.

Metope XXVII. 316. Figure 20. In dramatic force and boldness of composition this is one of the finest of the surviving metopes. The centaur is wounded and turns to flee, while he presses the wound in his back with his right hand. The Lapith holds him back and, grasping the side of his head, is about to deliver a second thrust. His body stands out against the folds of his cloak. The centaur's tail was omitted by the sculptor. The Lapith's head is in Athens.

Metope XXVIII. 317. Figure 21. Another fine and dramatic composition. The centaur's left arm is wrapped in a panther-skin, of which

fig 22 The East Pediment of the Parthenon in 1674 (from a drawing by Jacques
Carrey, in the Bibliothèque Nationale, Paris)

the tail and one paw stream out behind; he rushes forward exultingly over his opponent, whose body is relaxed in death. The centaur was holding some missile on his right shoulder: its remains suggest that it was a large bowl.

Metope XXIX. 318. An elderly centaur is making off with a young Lapith girl.

Metope XXX. 319. The centaur treads down the Lapith, whose strength is evidently failing: with his left hand he feebly clutches a stone. No hair is indicated on the centaur's tail; unless the tail is unfinished, this detail must have been supplied by the painter.

Metope XXXI. 320. The centaur is trying to throw the Lapith by grappling his right leg. This is a wrestling hold, no doubt familiar to the sculptor from contests in Athens. It is evident that the centaur has the advantage and that the Lapith is on the point of being thrown. The centaur's head is of a grotesque type, and contrasts with the humane, almost benevolent, head of the centaur on Metope XXX.

Metope XXXII. 321. The last (most easterly) metope of the South side of the temple. The centaur had seized the back of the Lapith's head with his left hand and was drawing back his right hand to strike, at the same time trying to grip him with his legs. The Lapith seems to have been striking with his right hand.

THE EAST PEDIMENT The subject of the East Pediment was the BIRTH OF ATHENA. This curious, primitive legend, of which the earliest extant version is given by the poet Hesiod (about 700 BC), described how the head of Zeus was cleft by Hephaestus (or Prometheus), whereupon Athena leapt from it fully armed. Whatever its meaning — and it has been much discussed[1] — this is obviously a difficult subject to present with

[1] The legend was that Zeus had previously swallowed his first consort Metis (Wisdom) whilst she was with child; and, since one of the chief attributes of Athena is wisdom, the meaning may be that it is part of, and proceeds from, the supreme God.

42

dignity. The painters of archaic Greek vases did not hesitate to show a tiny doll-like figure actually emerging from the head of Zeus; but the designer of the East Pediment chose the moment after the event, and showed Athena, on a scale slightly smaller than her father, springing away to one side. The central group of the pediment with this scene perished many centuries ago, probably about AD 450, when the Parthenon was converted into a Christian church and an apse was built at its East end. This created the 40-foot gap which can be seen in Carrey's drawing of 1674 (*fig 22*): but we possess some evidence of how the scene was composed, the most important being the circular altar now in Madrid, sometimes called the Madrid 'puteal' (well-head) because it was later put to this use. This was made in Roman times (first or second century AD): it is carved with figures in relief (*fig 23*); and there is little doubt that some, if not all, reproduce figures from the East Pediment. Thus in the centre was Zeus, seated, a figure more than ten feet high: in front of him the newly born Athena: between them Victory flying forward to crown her, and, behind Zeus, Hephaestus stepping aside with the axe in his hand. There are strong grounds for believing that to the left of Hephaestus were set figures like the remaining three on the altar in Madrid: if arranged to the left of the central scene they could fit the

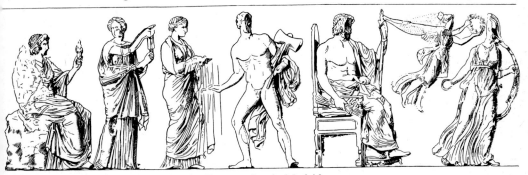

fig 23 Relief sculpture from a circular Roman altar in Madrid: THE THREE FATES.
HEPHAESTUS, ZEUS, NIKE, ATHENA

narrowing field of the pediment, and there, as on the altar, would be the Three Fates, whom the Greeks believed to preside at every birth. The missing figures immediately to the right of Athena cannot be reconstructed with certainty, but Carrey's drawings provide excellent evidence for the position of the sculptures from each corner of the pediment. We begin with the left (South) end, and see the head and arms of a man rising from a slab of marble on which ripples are carved (A): he is HELIOS, the sun-god, driving his chariot up out of the sea as day breaks: in front are the heads of two of the four horses of his team (B, C)[1].

Facing Helios is a male figure (D, *fig 24*) seated on the skin of a panther or a lion: this, and his position in the pediment, are almost the only clues to his identity. If the skin is that of a lion, he may be HERACLES, the hero who, with Athena's help, was to win immortality by his labours, the first of which was the killing of the Nemean lion. By some he has been thought to personify MOUNT OLYMPUS (which would serve to indicate the place in which the central event

[1] The other two heads are in Athens.

fig 24 East Pediment, DIONYSUS (*photograph,* James Mortimer)

fig 25 East Pediment, PERSEPHONE, DEMETER, HEBE (*photograph,* James Mortimer)

occurred, as the rising sun indicates the time): by others DIONYSUS, the wine-god, who commonly carries a panther-skin and would be an appropriate neighbour for the next two figures (E, F, *fig 25*), whose identity is fairly certain. They are DEMETER, goddess of the grain-bearing earth, and her daughter PERSEPHONE, goddess of the growing wheat, though which is which we cannot be sure: probably Demeter is nearer to the centre of the pediment. They sit on chests, which are covered with folded cloths, that to the right also with a skin or leather rug: chests and elaborately woven or embroidered cloths were used in the ritual of these goddesses, and the skin may be an allusion to Demeter's connexion with horses: whilst as an earth-goddess who was the constant benefactress of mankind she would be regarded as an appropriate intermediary between Zeus and the world of men. She stretches out her arm to a young girl running towards her (G, *fig 25*), whose drapery billows out behind: the girl is not winged; and this makes it likely that she is not Iris, the messenger of the gods, but perhaps HEBE, the cup-bearer of Zeus, starting back in alarm at the miraculous event which has just taken place.

The first figure preserved on the right of the central gap (K) was looking towards the centre and therefore away from the two beside her (L, M), but it is common to regard all three as a single group: like these two outer figures, who rest on a long rock covered with

45

fig 26 East Pediment, HESTIA, DIONE, APHRODITE (*photograph,* James Mortimer)

drapery, she, too, is seated on a rock similarly covered, although it and she are carved from another block of marble (*fig 26*). The old identification of the three figures as the Fates must now be given up, since it is clear that the Fates were shown in another part of the pediment (see above, p. 44): a better suggestion is, however, not easy. Some which have been made are: for the goddess on the left– HESTIA: for the two on the right–THALASSA (the Sea) in the lap of GAIA (the Earth), or APHRODITE in the lap of her mother DIONE: for the three together–the CLOUDS, or the HESPERID NYMPHS, daughters of Night, at the most westerly confines of the world. There is no doubt about the sculptures in the extreme angle of the pediment: Selene, goddess of the Moon, was shown sinking below the horizon in her four-horse chariot: of the goddess only the upper part from the waist was still to be seen, and all but the heads of the horses had sunk out of sight. The horse's head here preserved (o, *fig 27*) is a masterpiece in its rendering of essential forms; its tiredness, subtly expressed, forms a contrast with the freshness of the Sun's team in the far corner of the pediment. The torso of Selene (the head missing) is in Athens, as are two of the remaining horses' heads, much defaced: the fourth is lost.

North Slip Room

This room contains fragments of sculpture and architecture from the Parthenon.

46

IV. BIBLIOGRAPHY

(Many books and articles have been written about the Parthenon: a few only can be mentioned here.)

Architecture

F. PENROSE, *Principles of Athenian Architecture*, London (1888, 2nd edition). Penrose was the first to discover, measure, and describe in detail the extraordinary 'refinements' with which the Parthenon was built. He also recorded the traces of colour.

The architecture of the Parthenon is briefly treated in standard hand-books such as:
W. B. DINSMOOR, *The Architecture of Ancient Greece*, London (3rd edition, 1950).
D. S. ROBERTSON, *A Hand-book of Greek and Roman Architecture*, Cambridge (2nd edition, 1945).

G. P. STEVENS, 'The Periclean Entrance-court of the Acropolis of Athens', *Hesperia*, V (1936). Research into the architectural setting and surroundings of the Parthenon.
G. P. STEVENS, 'The Setting of the Periclean Parthenon', *Hesperia*, Supplement III (1940).
G. P. STEVENS, 'Architectural Studies Concerning the Acropolis of Athens', *Hesperia*, XV (1946). Contains a good bird's-eye view of a reconstruction of the Acropolis.
W. B. DINSMOOR, 'The Hekatompedon on the Athenian Acropolis', *American Journal of Archaeology*, LI (1947). Deals with the earlier buildings on the site of the Parthenon.
G. P. STEVENS, *Restorations of Classical Buildings*, Princeton (1958).

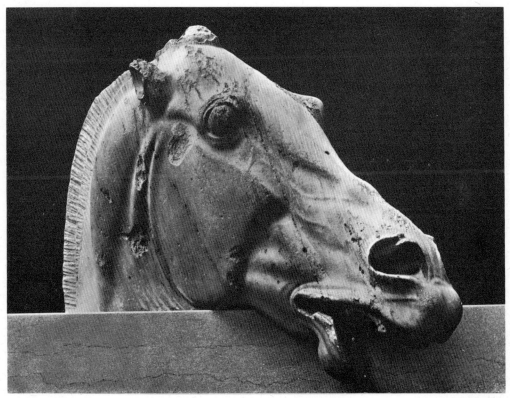

fig 27 East Pediment, HORSE OF SELENE (*photograph*, James Mortimer)

Architecture and Sculpture

M. COLLIGNON, *Le Parthénon*, Paris (1912). In French. Excellent account of the history, architecture, and sculpture. Many large plates.

W. HEGE and G. RODENWALDT, *The Acropolis*, Oxford (1932). A good picture-book, which includes forty plates of the Parthenon.

Sculpture

A. H. SMITH, *The Sculptures of the Parthenon*, London (1910). This is the main publication of the marbles preserved in the British Museum: it also contains details of all other fragments of sculpture recognized at the time of its publication as belonging to the Parthenon. Many large plates.

P. E. CORBETT, *The Sculpture of the Parthenon*, Penguin Books, Harmondsworth (1959).

N. YALOURIS and F. L. KENETT, *Classical Greece. The Sculpture of the Parthenon*, London (1960).

F. BROMMER, *Die Skulpturen der Parthenon-Giebel*, Mainz (1963).

F. BROMMER, *Die Giebel des Parthenon*, Mainz (1959).

RHYS CARPENTER, 'New Material for the West Pediment of the Parthenon', *Hesperia*, I (1932).

RHYS CARPENTER, 'The Lost Statues of the East Pediment of the Parthenon', *Hesperia*, II (1933).

Athena Parthenos

F. BROMMER, *Athena Parthenos*, Opus Nobile 11, Bremen (1957).

C. J. HERINGTON, *Athena Parthenos and Athena Polias*, Manchester (1955).

Building-accounts

A. M. WOODWARD, 'Some new Fragments of Attic Building-records', *Annual of the British School at Athens*, XVI (1909–10).

W. B. DINSMOOR, 'Attic Building-accounts', *American Journal of Archaeology*, XVII (1913), and XXV (1921).

Lord Elgin and his Collection

'Report from the Select Committee on the Earl of Elgin's Collection', House of Commons, 1816.

A. H. SMITH, 'Lord Elgin and his Collection', *Journal of Hellenic Studies*, XXXVI (1916).